UNLUCKING *YOUR* CHILD'S POTENTIAL

Transforming challenges into strengths in children with high-functioning autism

MIKE BUCK

WHY I THIS BOOK

Have you ever gazed at a kaleidoscope, mesmerized by the way a single twist explodes into a symphony of color and intricate patterns? That's how I see the world of children with High-Functioning Autism (HFA). They possess unique perspectives that paint the world in vibrant hues, notice details most miss, and approach learning with a laser focus.

But sometimes, that same brilliant light can feel like a spotlight, illuminating challenges that can be overwhelming. Social interactions might feel like navigating a foreign language, sensory overload can threaten to drown out the world, and the desire for routine can clash with the chaos of everyday life.

That's where the inspiration for **Unlocking Your Child's Potential** bloomed. It wasn't just about managing challenges; it was about celebrating the extraordinary strengths hidden within these unique minds. I wanted to create a book that empowered parents and caregivers a roadmap to navigate this beautiful and complex landscape.

Think of it as a secret decoder ring, helping you understand your child's nonverbal cues. Or a toolbox filled with practical strategies to transform anxieties into strengths and social awkwardness into endearing quirks.

Unlocking Your Child's Potential is more than just a book; it's a whispered promise. A promise to parents that they're not alone. A promise to children that their unique way of seeing the world is a gift to be cherished, not a challenge to be overcome. It's about unlocking the potential within, celebrating the kaleidoscope of colors, and embarking on a journey of discovery together.

So, are you ready to join the adventure?

DEDICATION

This book is dedicated to all the children on the Autism Spectrum, particularly those with High-Functioning Autism. Your unique perspectives illuminate the world with a kaleidoscope of colors and a fascination for detail. You remind us that there is beauty in seeing things differently, and that true strength lies in embracing your individuality.

May this story inspire you to celebrate your unique talents, build bridges of understanding, and embark on a lifelong journey of discovery.

With love and admiration,

ACKNOWLEDGMENTS

The journey of bringing this book to life wouldn't have been possible without the invaluable contributions of many remarkable individuals.

First and foremost, my deepest gratitude goes to the incredible community of parents, caregivers, and professionals working tirelessly to support children with High-Functioning Autism. Your dedication, resilience, and unwavering love inspire me every day.

Special thanks to the following individuals who played a crucial role in shaping this book:

- ***The Autism Spectrum Community:*** *Thank you to the families who shared their stories, experiences, and insights. Your voices provided invaluable guidance and a deeper understanding of the triumphs and challenges faced by children with HFA.*

- ***The Experts:*** *My heartfelt appreciation to the educators, therapists, and medical professionals who generously shared their expertise. Your knowledge and guidance helped ensure the accuracy and comprehensiveness of the information presented.*

- ***My Support System:*** *A warm thank you to my friends and family for their unwavering encouragement, patience, and understanding throughout the writing process. Your support fueled my passion and kept me motivated.*

Finally, a special note of thanks to (mention any specific editors, collaborators, or people who helped with the creative process). Your contributions were instrumental in bringing this book to fruition.

Thank you all for believing in the power of this story and for your commitment to unlocking the potential of every child.

Mike Buck

TABLE OF CONTENTS

INTRODUCTION

Does Your Child See the World Differently? Welcome to the Thriving Realm of Neurodiversity!

Does your child light up at the flutter of a butterfly's wing but struggle in noisy environments? Do they excel in areas that amaze you, yet sometimes have social interactions that leave you feeling confused? If so, your child might be neurodiverse, and that's a cause for celebration!

This book is your empowering guide to navigating the beautiful world of neurodiversity, specifically high-functioning autism. We'll move beyond diagnoses and labels to focus on unlocking your child's unique potential. Imagine a future where your child thrives, embraces their individuality, and reaches their full potential.

This book is your roadmap to get there. Let's embark on this journey together, where we'll explore:

- *The strengths and superpowers that come with neurodiversity.*

- *Strategies to navigate social challenges and sensory sensitivities.*

- *Effective communication techniques to build strong connections.*

- *The power of collaboration: working with educators, therapists, and family to create a supportive network.*

- *And most importantly, fostering your child's self-esteem and celebrating their unique path.*

This book is filled with practical tools, inspiring stories, and expert insights to help you understand, nurture, and empower your neurodiverse child.

Get ready to unlock a world of possibilities and celebrate the incredible journey ahead!

PART 1

BUILDING A STRONG FOUNDATION

Welcome to Part 1 of our journey to unlocking your child's potential! In this section, we'll delve into the essential building blocks for a strong and fulfilling relationship between a child with High-Functioning Autism (HFA) and their loved ones.

Just like any magnificent structure, a strong relationship needs a solid foundation. Here, we'll explore three key cornerstones that will pave the way for connection and communication:

- Establishing Trust: This chapter dives into the importance of trust as the bedrock of any meaningful relationship. We'll explore strategies for building trust and fostering a safe space for open communication.

- Creating a Predictable World: For children with HFA, a predictable environment can feel comforting and secure. This chapter explores strategies for creating routines, providing clear expectations, and minimizing surprises to promote a sense of well-being and reduce anxiety.

- Decoding Communication Challenges: Communication can sometimes feel like a puzzle, especially when interacting with someone who sees the world differently. This chapter will equip you with strategies for understanding communication challenges that might arise and bridge the gap for smoother interaction.

By focusing on these cornerstones, you can create a nurturing environment where your child feels safe, understood, and empowered to connect with the world around them.

So, let's embark on this journey together and build a strong foundation for a lifetime of love, communication, and understanding!

CHAPTER 2: BUILDING BRIDGES: FOSTERING CONNECTION AND COMMUNICATION

The world of communication can feel like a bustling marketplace when you have a child with High-Functioning Autism (HFA). Understanding their unique way of processing information and expressing themselves can sometimes feel like deciphering a secret code. But within this challenge lies a beautiful opportunity to build a bridge of connection and understanding. This chapter dives deep into the cornerstones that foster a strong and supportive relationship: establishing trust, creating a predictable world, and decoding communication challenges.

2.1 Establishing Trust: The Cornerstone of a Strong Relationship

Trust is the bedrock of any meaningful relationship, and even more so when navigating the complexities of autism. For a child with HFA, the world can feel unpredictable and overwhelming. They may struggle with social nuances and sensory sensitivities, creating a constant undercurrent of anxiety. A foundation of trust is essential for them to feel safe enough to lower their defenses and truly connect.

Here's how you can build a foundation of trust with your child:

- **Be Reliable and Consistent:** Children with HFA thrive on consistency. Follow through on promises, maintain consistent routines as much as possible, and strive to be a dependable source of comfort and support.

This predictability creates a sense of security and allows them to focus on communication and connection.

- **Active Listening:** Words are powerful, but active listening is the true magic trick. Give your child your undivided attention when they communicate, whether verbally or nonverbally. Make eye contact at their comfort level, put away distractions like your phone, and show genuine interest in what they have to say. Acknowledge their emotions by reflecting their feelings back to them (e.g., "I see you're feeling frustrated right now. Can you tell me what's bothering you?").

- **Respecting Boundaries:** Pay close attention to your child's cues. If they seem overwhelmed by social interaction or need quiet time, respect their need for space.

Pushing them beyond their comfort zone can erode trust and create unnecessary anxiety. Creating a safe haven, like a designated quiet space in the home, allows them to retreat and recharge when needed.

- **Honesty and Transparency:** Be honest and upfront with your child, even when delivering difficult news. Explain things in a way they can understand, avoiding sugarcoating or minimizing their concerns. Use age-appropriate language and avoid making promises you can't keep. Broken promises can shatter trust and make them hesitant to communicate openly in the future.
- **Celebrating Small Victories:** Every step forward, no matter how small, deserves recognition.

Acknowledge and celebrate your child's efforts in building communication skills, expressing emotions, or navigating social situations. Positive reinforcement builds confidence and strengthens the bond between you. Celebrate their successes, both big and small, to show them that their efforts are valued.

Building trust is an ongoing process, not a one-time achievement. By consistently demonstrating these qualities, you create a safe space where your child feels comfortable expressing themselves openly and honestly. This, in turn, fosters a strong foundation for a lifetime of love, communication, and understanding.

2.2 Creating a Predictable World: Building a Safe and Supportive Environment

Imagine your child's world as a vibrant kaleidoscope. While beautiful, it can also be overwhelming. The sights, sounds, and social interactions that seem commonplace to us can feel chaotic and unpredictable for a child with HFA. Creating a predictable world becomes crucial in fostering a sense of security and promoting emotional well-being.

Here are some strategies to create a predictable and supportive environment:

- **Visual Schedules:** Visual aids, like pictures or charts, can be immensely helpful. Create visual schedules that outline daily routines, upcoming events, and transitions throughout the day.

This provides a clear understanding of what to expect, reducing anxiety associated with the unknown. You can create these schedules together, allowing your child to participate and feel a sense of control.

- **Clear Expectations:** Set clear and consistent expectations for behavior at home and in different social situations. Use simple language with positive reinforcement to encourage desired behaviors (e.g., "When we go to the store, we use quiet voices and walk beside each other"). Avoid relying on vague instructions that might be misinterpreted.

- **Minimize Surprises:** Whenever possible, prepare your child for upcoming changes, like a new haircut, a doctor's appointment, or a playdate. Explain what to expect in simple terms, allowing them to mentally adjust and feel more in control.

- **Sensory Sensitivities:** Be mindful of your child's sensory sensitivities. If they are particularly sensitive to loud noises, bright lights, or certain textures, adapt the environment accordingly. Provide noise-canceling headphones, offer sunglasses in bright environments, or allow them to wear comfortable clothing that feels soothing.

- **Quiet Spaces**: Dedicate a quiet space in your home where your child can retreat to escape overwhelming sensory experiences or simply relax. This could be a cozy reading nook, a sensory tent, or even a specific corner of their bedroom. Make sure this space is comfortable and provides a sense of security.

The Power of Routine

Routines are more than just daily schedules; they provide a sense of order and control for a child with HFA. Knowing what to expect throughout the day reduces anxiety and allows them to focus their energy on communication and social interaction. Here are some tips for creating effective routines:

- Morning and Bedtime Routines: Establish consistent routines for waking up, getting ready for school, bedtime, and any other regular activities. This predictability promotes a sense of calm and allows them to transition smoothly between activities.
- Visual Cues: Complement routines with visual cues like picture charts or timers. This provides a visual reminder of upcoming steps and helps them anticipate what comes next.

- Choice and Flexibility: While routines are important, some flexibility can be beneficial. Offer your child small choices within the routine (e.g., letting them choose their outfit for the day within a pre-selected wardrobe) to foster a sense of independence and control.

Predictability doesn't have to mean rigidity. Unexpected events will inevitably arise. The key is to prepare your child as much as possible and offer support during these times. By creating a predictable and supportive environment, you equip your child with a sense of security and control, allowing them to feel more comfortable venturing into unfamiliar social situations and engaging in meaningful communication.

2.3 Decoding Communication Challenges: Strategies for Understanding and Connecting

Communication with a child with HFA can sometimes feel like trying to solve a puzzle with missing pieces. They may struggle with verbal expression, take things very literally, or misinterpret social cues. But with a little effort and understanding, you can bridge the gap and foster meaningful connections. Here are some strategies to decode communication challenges:

- Understanding Nonverbal Cues: Children with HFA often rely heavily on nonverbal communication. Pay attention to their body language, facial expressions, and tone of voice. A furrowed brow might indicate frustration, clenched fists could signal anxiety, and excited jumping might express joy. Learning to read these nonverbal cues allows you to better understand their true feelings and needs.

- Focus on Interests: Use your child's passions as a springboard for communication. Talk about their favorite topics, engage in shared activities related to their interests (building Legos, drawing superheroes), and use these interactions to build rapport and understanding.

- Literal Interpretation: Children with HFA may take things very literally. Avoid sarcasm, figurative language, and double meanings, as they might be misinterpreted. Communicate in clear and concise language, avoiding complex sentences and jargon. Break down information into smaller, manageable pieces to ensure they understand the message.

- Simple Language: Less is often more when communicating with a child with HFA. Use simple, direct language and avoid overwhelming them with too much information at once. Focus on one concept at a time and give them time to process what you've said before moving on.

- Visual Aids: Visual aids can be powerful tools for communication and understanding. Use pictures, symbols, or social stories to explain concepts, social situations, and expected behaviors. Social stories, in particular, can be helpful in preparing your child for upcoming events like a school play, a visit to the dentist, or a family gathering.

- Patience and Empathy: Building communication skills takes time and patience. Celebrate your child's efforts, no matter how small.

Avoid getting frustrated if they don't always express themselves in a typical way. Remember, they are constantly learning and developing their communication skills. Empathy is key. Try to see the world from their perspective and understand the challenges they might be facing.

Building the Bridge of Communication

Communication is a two-way street. By utilizing these strategies, you can create a space where your child feels comfortable expressing themselves openly and honestly. Actively listen to their thoughts and feelings, respond with empathy, and encourage them to ask questions. This back-and-forth interaction builds trust, strengthens your bond, and paves the way for a lifetime of meaningful communication.

Remember, you are not alone on this journey. There are many resources available to help you on your parenting journey with a child with HFA. Support groups, online communities, and professional guidance can provide invaluable tools and strategies.

The road ahead may have its bumps and detours, but with a foundation of trust, a predictable environment, and a willingness to decode communication challenges, you can build a strong and lasting bridge of connection with your child. This bridge will not only foster understanding and communication but also pave the way for a world of love, acceptance,

This chapter equips you with the tools to build a strong foundation for communication and connection with your child.

The next chapters will delve deeper into specific strategies for navigating social interactions, managing challenging behaviors, and unlocking your child's full

PART 2

CONQUERING CHALLENGES: EQUIPPING YOUR CHILD FOR SOCIAL SUCCESS

Does navigating social interactions sometimes feel like a complex maze for your child? You want them to connect with others, but social cues can be confusing, and emotions can run high. Don't worry, you're not alone! Part 2: Conquering Challenges dives into the social and emotional landscape often encountered by children with high-functioning autism. We'll equip you with tools to:

- **Crack the code of nonverbal communication:** Help your child understand facial expressions, body language, and social cues that might otherwise be missed.

- **Navigate tantrums and anxiety outbursts:** Discover practical strategies for managing emotions and fostering calm communication.

- **Build social skills and empathy:** Empower your child to connect with others, build friendships, and thrive in social settings.

Together, we'll transform these perceived barriers into opportunities for growth and empower your child to navigate the social world with confidence. So, take a deep breath, adventurer it's time to conquer the maze and celebrate social success!

CHAPTER 3: MASTERING THE SOCIAL MAZE: UNDERSTANDING AND MANAGING SOCIAL AND EMOTIONAL DIFFICULTIES

The social world can be a vibrant and exciting place, but for children with high-functioning autism, it can sometimes feel like a complex maze. Social cues might feel like cryptic messages, emotional responses might seem out of proportion, and navigating interactions can be overwhelming. This chapter is your guide to becoming a master navigator of this social maze, equipping you with tools to understand and manage your child's social and emotional difficulties.

3.1 Recognizing Social Cues and Emotions: Cracking the Code of Nonverbal Communication

Imagine your child is at a friend's birthday party. They see a group of children laughing together,

but their body language seems closed off. They might be feeling left out, unsure how to join in. This section equips you with tools to help your child decipher the unspoken messages that influence social interactions:

- **Decoding Facial Expressions and Body Language:** Learn how to "read" facial expressions and body language, like crossed arms, furrowed brows, or a relaxed smile. Help your child understand the emotions these nonverbal cues might convey.

- **Understanding Tone of Voice:** Explore how tone of voice can drastically alter the meaning of words. Help your child distinguish playful teasing from genuine frustration to navigate interactions more effectively.

- **Social Scripts and Role-Playing:** Develop social scripts that outline appropriate responses for different situations. Role-play scenarios to practice these scripts in a safe and controlled environment.

- **Visual Aids:** Use social stories, pictures, or comic strips to visually represent social cues and expected behaviors, making them easier for your child to understand.

3.2 Taming the Tantrums: Practical Strategies for Managing Anxiety Outbursts

Meltdowns and anxiety outbursts can be a source of frustration for both you and your child. This section tackles strategies to manage these moments effectively:

- **Identifying Triggers:** Work together with your child to recognize situations, sensory experiences, or changes in routine that might trigger anxiety or emotional outbursts.

- **Developing a Communication Plan:** Create a plan for how your child can communicate their needs before frustration escalates. This could involve using picture cards, simple phrases, or nonverbal cues.

- **Calming Techniques and Sensory Tools:** Introduce calming techniques like deep breathing, counting, or sensory activities your child finds soothing (fidget toys, noise-canceling headphones, etc.). Practice these techniques regularly during calm moments for better effectiveness during meltdowns.

- **Positive Reinforcement:** Acknowledge and celebrate your child's efforts in managing their emotions and communicating their needs. This positive reinforcement encourages them to continue using these strategies.

3.3 Building Social Skills and Fostering Empathy: Helping Your Child Connect with Others

Social connections are vital for a child's emotional well-being and development.

This section equips you with tools to foster social skills and empathy in your child:

- **Conversational Skills:** Practice turn-taking, active listening, and maintaining eye contact during conversations. Introduce strategies for initiating conversations and appropriate topics for different social settings.

- **Navigating Play and Social Interactions:** Help your child understand social cues for joining playgroups, initiating interactions with peers, and taking turns during games.

- **Role-Playing and Social Activities:** Practice social skills through role-playing games and social activities tailored to your child's interests. This allows them to experiment with different social scenarios in a safe and supportive environment.

- **Developing Empathy:** Discuss the concept of empathy and why understanding others' feelings is important. Use books, movies, and real-life scenarios to help your child recognize and respond to the emotions of others.

Remember: Every child learns and progresses at their own pace. Be patient, celebrate small victories, and focus on building upon your child's strengths. With consistent effort and the strategies outlined in this chapter, you can empower your child to navigate the social world with confidence.

The next chapter delves deeper into the world of sensory sensitivities, exploring how these can impact your child and equipping you with tools for navigating this sensory landscape.

CHAPTER 4: NAVIGATING THE SENSORY WORLD: UNDERSTANDING AND SUPPORTING YOUR CHILD'S SENSORY NEEDS

The world is a symphony of sights, sounds, smells, textures, and tastes. While most of us process this sensory information seamlessly, for children with high-functioning autism, sensory experiences can be overwhelming or even painful. This chapter equips you with the tools to navigate this sensory world alongside your child, fostering understanding, and creating a supportive environment.

4.1 *Identifying Sensory Triggers: Understanding How Your Child Experiences the World*

Imagine a bustling school cafeteria. The bright overhead lights hum, the clatter of dishes fills the air, and the smell of cafeteria food lingers.

For some children, this environment might be stimulating and engaging. But for a child with sensory sensitivities, it could be overwhelming, leading to anxiety or meltdowns.

This section delves into the world of sensory processing and how it can impact your child:

- **Understanding the Senses:** Explore the eight sensory systems (auditory, visual, olfactory, gustatory, tactile, proprioception, vestibular, and interoception) and how they influence your child's experience of the world.

- **Identifying Sensory Triggers:** Learn to recognize signs of sensory overload, such as withdrawal, meltdowns, or fidgeting. Observe your child's reactions in different environments to identify specific triggers (loud noises, bright lights, certain textures, etc.).

- **Sensory Profiles:** While some children might be hypersensitive to certain stimuli (overstimulated easily), others might be hyposensitive (seeking more sensory input). Understanding your child's sensory profile is crucial for creating a supportive environment.

4.2 5 Sensory Integration Techniques to Calm and Focus Your Child

Sensory overload can lead to meltdowns and difficulty focusing. This section offers practical strategies to calm and refocus your child:

- **Movement Breaks:** Schedule regular movement breaks throughout the day to help your child release excess energy and refocus. This could involve jumping jacks, short walks, or deep breathing exercises.

- **Sensory Tools:** Introduce calming sensory tools that cater to your child's specific needs. This might include fidget toys, noise-canceling headphones, weighted blankets, chewy necklaces, or calming essential oils.

- **Creating a Calm Down Corner:** Establish a designated space in your home or classroom where your child can retreat during moments of sensory overload. Decorate it with calming colors and textures and equip it with sensory tools your child finds soothing.

- **Visual Schedules and Predictability:** Provide visual schedules or social stories to help your child anticipate upcoming transitions or changes in routine. This predictability can reduce anxiety and promote a sense of calm.

- **Positive Reinforcement:** Acknowledge and celebrate your child's efforts in self-regulating and using their sensory tools effectively.

4.3 *Adapting the Home and School Environment for Sensory Needs: Creating a Sensory-Friendly Space*

Our environments can significantly impact how we experience the world. This section explores ways to adapt your home and school environment to support your child's sensory needs:

- **Lighting:** Consider using dimmer switches or providing natural light sources to adjust brightness levels.

- **Sound Management:** Minimize background noise by using white noise machines or earplugs when needed.

- **Tactile Considerations:** Offer a variety of textures for your child to explore, such as soft blankets, textured toys, or play dough.

- **Creating Designated Areas:** Create dedicated areas for activities that might require different sensory experiences (quiet reading corner, calming space, energetic play area).

- **Collaborating with Educators:** Work with your child's teachers to create a sensory-friendly environment in the classroom. This might involve providing fidget tools, establishing a quiet area for breaks, or offering alternative activities during overwhelming situations.

Remember: Every child experience sensory input differently. Experimenting with different strategies and creating a sensory-friendly environment tailored to your child's specific needs is key to promoting calmness, focus, and a sense of well-being.

The next chapter dives into the world of executive functioning, exploring how these skills impact learning and daily life, and equipping you with strategies to empower your child.

CHAPTER 5: EXECUTIVE FUNCTIONING: EMPOWERING YOUR CHILD TO TAKE CHARGE

Imagine a conductor leading an orchestra. They plan the music, organize the instruments, and ensure everyone plays their part to create a harmonious symphony. In the world of learning and daily life, executive functioning skills play a similar role. This chapter explores these crucial skills and equips you with tools to empower your child to become the conductor of their own success.

5.1 Understanding Executive Functioning and its Impact on Learning

Executive functioning (EF) is a set of mental skills that help us plan, organize, focus, and manage our time effectively. These skills are essential for success in school, work, and daily life.

However, for children with high-functioning autism, EF can be a challenge, impacting their ability to learn and thrive in certain environments.

This section delves deeper into the key elements of EF and how they influence learning:

- **Working Memory:** Imagine holding onto information in your mind while you complete a task. Weak working memory can make it difficult for your child to follow multi-step instructions or complete complex tasks.

- **Organization and Planning:** Planning out a homework assignment or organizing school supplies requires organizational skills. Difficulties in this area can lead to procrastination and disorganization.

- **Time Management:** Knowing how to manage time effectively is crucial for completing tasks within deadlines.

Children with weak time management skills might struggle to stay on track and finish projects on time.

- **Metacognition:** "Thinking about thinking" allows us to monitor our own progress and adjust our strategies as needed. Weak metacognition might make it difficult for your child to recognize when they're stuck or need to adjust their approach to a problem.

Understanding these challenges is the first step to supporting your child's development and learning.

5.2 Strategies for Improving Organization, Planning, and Time Management: Building Time Management Muscles

Just like any muscle, executive functioning skills can be strengthened with practice and the right strategies.

This section equips you with tools to help your child improve their organizational skills, planning abilities, and time management:

- **Visual Aids and Checklists:** Create visual schedules, checklists, and to-do lists to break down large tasks into manageable steps. This provides a clear roadmap and helps your child stay organized.

- **Timers and Alarms:** Utilize timers and alarms to help your child stay on track and manage time effectively during homework sessions or daily routines.

- **Planning and Prioritization:** Teach your child the importance of planning and prioritizing tasks. Help them break down large projects into smaller, more manageable steps and prioritize tasks based on deadlines or importance.

- **Organizing Tools:** Provide organizational tools like binders, folders, and color-coded systems to help your child keep track of schoolwork and belongings.

- **Positive Reinforcement:** Acknowledge and celebrate your child's efforts in using organizational tools and managing their time effectively. This positive reinforcement encourages them to continue using these strategies.

5.3 Building Problem-Solving and Decision-Making Skills: Equipping Your Child for Success

Navigating daily life requires making decisions and solving problems. This section explores strategies to empower your child in these areas:

- **Brainstorming and Creative Solutions:** Encourage your child to brainstorm different solutions when faced with problems. Role-playing different scenarios can help them explore various options and reach a decision.

- **Cause-and-Effect Thinking:** Help your child understand the cause and effect of their actions. This allows them to make informed decisions and anticipate potential consequences.

- **Critical Thinking and Logic:** Foster critical thinking skills by asking open-ended questions and encouraging your child to analyze situations logically before making decisions.

- **Step-by-Step Problem Solving:** Break down complex problems into smaller, more manageable steps. Guide your child through the process of analyzing the problem, identifying potential solutions, and evaluating the best course of action.

Remember: Developing strong executive functioning skills takes time and consistent effort. Be patient, celebrate your child's progress, and focus on building upon their strengths. With the strategies outlined in this chapter, you can empower your child to become an effective planner, a skilled organizer, and a confident decision-maker.

In the next Part delves into the world of self-advocacy and self-awareness, empowering your child to communicate their needs and navigate life with confidence.

PART 3

PROMOTING POSITIVE DEVELOPMENT: EMPOWERING YOUR CHILD TO SHINE

Your child's journey with high-functioning autism is unique, filled with strengths, passions, and a desire to thrive. This section equips you with tools to unlock their full potential:

Unleashing Creativity: Discover your child's hidden talents, nurture their passions, and foster a love for creative expression.

Building Independence: Empower your child to advocate for themselves, manage daily tasks, and navigate life with confidence.

Building Friendships: Foster healthy social connections, equip your child with the skills to build friendships, and navigate social situations with ease.

We'll explore strategies to help your child:

- Identify their strengths and passions.
- Express themselves creatively and explore their interests.
- Speak up for themselves and manage their needs effectively.
- Develop meaningful friendships and navigate social interactions confidently.
- Get ready to celebrate your child's unique journey as they blossom and thrive!

CHAPTER 6: UNLEASHING CREATIVITY: STRATEGIES TO HELP YOUR CHILD THRIVE IN THEIR PASSIONS

Every child possesses a spark of creativity waiting to be ignited. For children with high-functioning autism, this spark can sometimes be overshadowed by challenges. This chapter is your guide to fanning that spark into a flame, helping you identify your child's unique strengths and passions, and fostering a love for creative expression.

6.1 Identifying Your Child's Strengths and Passions: Discovering Hidden Talents

Uncovering your child's hidden talents is like embarking on a treasure hunt. Here are some tools to help you navigate this exciting journey:

- **Become an Observer:** Be a keen observer of your child's activities and interests. Do they light up when drawing, building elaborate structures with blocks, or getting lost in a good book? Pay attention to their natural curiosity and the activities that bring them joy.

- **Embrace Repetitive Behaviors:** While repetitive behaviors can sometimes be a source of concern, they can also be a sign of deep focus and passion. Channel these behaviors into creative outlets. For instance, a child who enjoys lining up objects could explore intricate beadwork patterns or create mesmerizing stop-motion animation.

- **Shift the Focus:** Move your focus from challenges to strengths. When you celebrate your child's natural abilities, you empower them to build confidence and explore areas where they excel.

- **Offer a Buffet of Experiences:** Provide your child with opportunities to explore a variety of activities and hobbies. Sign them up for a class, visit museums or art galleries, or simply create a space at home for them to tinker and experiment. This broadens their horizons and allows them to discover new passions they might not have known existed.

6.2 *Building Upon Natural Abilities and Fostering Creativity*

Once you've identified your child's passions, it's time to nurture them and watch their creativity flourish! Here are some strategies to cultivate a thriving creative environment:

- **Create a Supportive Space:** Dedicate a space in your home for your child to explore their passions. This could be an art studio stocked with paints and brushes, a quiet reading nook, or a music corner with instruments.

- **The Power of Play:** Play is not just fun; it's a springboard for creativity. Encourage imaginative play, storytelling, or collaborative art projects. Engage in activities that spark their interests and allow them to explore their passions freely.

- **Embrace the Imperfect:** Shift the focus from achieving a perfect end product to enjoying the creative process. Encourage your child to experiment, take risks, and embrace imperfections as a natural part of the artistic journey. Celebrate the joy of creation and the unique perspective they bring to their work.

- **Celebrate Every Milestone:** Acknowledge and celebrate your child's efforts, big and small. Did they finally master a difficult piano piece? Did they create a story they're particularly proud of? Celebrate these achievements, no matter how seemingly insignificant, as they fuel their motivation to keep exploring.

- **Find a Tribe:** Seek out mentors or communities that share your child's interests. This allows them to connect with like-minded individuals, learn from experienced mentors, and build a supportive network that celebrates their creativity.

6.3 Encouraging Independence and Self-Advocacy Skills: Empowering Your Child to Speak Up

As your child delves deeper into their passions, fostering independence becomes crucial.

Here are some ways to empower them to advocate for their needs and manage their creative endeavors:

- **Age-Appropriate Responsibilities:** Assign age-appropriate chores and responsibilities related to their hobbies.

This could involve cleaning their art supplies, keeping their music practice space organized, or planning their own creative projects. This instills a sense of ownership and independence.

- **Communication is Key:** Help your child develop communication skills to express their needs and preferences related to their passions. For example, if they need specific art supplies or prefer a quiet environment to write, encourage them to voice those needs confidently. Role-playing scenarios can help them practice assertive communication.

- **Empowering Decisions:** Guide your child through the decision-making process as they explore their creative pursuits. Encourage them to consider different options, weigh the pros and cons, and make choices related to their hobbies and creative endeavors.

This empowers them to take ownership of their creative journey.

By fostering creativity, you unlock a world of self-expression, joy, and confidence for your child. As they delve into their passions, develop self-advocacy skills, and gain independence, they become empowered to embrace their unique talents and thrive in a world that celebrates their individuality.

The next chapter dives into the world of social connection, exploring strategies to foster meaningful friendships and navigate social interactions with confidence.

CHAPTER 7: BUILDING FRIENDSHIPS: FOSTERING HEALTHY RELATIONSHIPS

Friendships are the cornerstones of a fulfilling life, providing us with a sense of belonging, support, and joy. For children with high-functioning autism, navigating the complexities of social interaction and building friendships can sometimes feel like a daunting task.

This chapter equips you with tools to empower your child to build strong social connections and foster healthy relationships with their peers.

7.1 Understanding the Importance of Friendships and Social Interaction: The Power of Connection

Imagine a world where your child feels a sense of belonging, has someone to share their joys and sorrows with, and experiences the laughter and camaraderie of true friendship. Friendships provide a multitude of benefits, including:

- **Social and Emotional Development:** Friendships help children develop social skills, empathy, and emotional intelligence. Through interaction with peers, they learn to communicate effectively, navigate social cues, and build self-confidence.

- **A Sense of Belonging:** Feeling accepted and valued by peers fosters a sense of belonging and self-worth. Friendships provide a safe space for children to be themselves and connect with others who share their interests.

- **Resilience and Support:** Friends offer a supportive network, helping children navigate challenges, cope with setbacks, and celebrate successes. Strong friendships can act as a buffer against stress and anxiety.

- **Enhanced Learning and Exploration:** Friends often engage in shared activities and explore new interests together. This collaborative learning environment can enhance academic performance and broaden a child's horizons.

By fostering friendships, you open a door to a world of social connection and emotional well-being for your child.

7.2 Helping Your Child Make and Maintain Friendships: Building Social Bridges

Building friendships doesn't happen overnight. It requires dedication, effort, and the development of essential social skills. Here are some strategies to guide your child on this journey:

- **Identify Potential Friends:** Help your child identify potential friends who share similar interests. This could involve looking for classmates who enjoy the same hobbies or participating in social groups or clubs that cater to your child's passions.

- **Practice Social Skills:** Role-play social scenarios like initiating conversations, joining group activities, or asking someone to play. This allows your child to practice their social skills in a safe and controlled environment.

- **Social Communication Strategies:** Equip your child with strategies for initiating conversations, maintaining eye contact, and using appropriate greetings. Social stories can also be helpful tools for explaining social situations and expected behaviors.

- **Embrace Shared Activities:** Encourage participation in activities and hobbies that allow your child to interact with peers who share their interests. This creates a natural springboard for conversation and social connection.

- **Positive Reinforcement:** Acknowledge and celebrate your child's efforts in initiating friendships and engaging in social interactions. This positive reinforcement motivates them to continue developing their social skills.

7.3 Managing Conflict Resolution and Social Challenges with Peers: Navigating Social Conflicts

Disagreements and misunderstandings are inevitable in any friendship. Here are some strategies to help your child navigate social conflicts with peers:

- **Understanding Nonverbal Cues:** Help your child recognize nonverbal cues that might indicate frustration or anger in others. This allows them to identify potential conflicts before they escalate.

- **Communication and Compromise:** Teach your child assertive communication skills to express their needs and feelings effectively. Encourage them to find solutions through compromise and collaboration.

- **De-escalation Techniques:** Equip your child with calming strategies to manage their emotions during conflicts. This could involve deep breathing exercises, taking a short break from the situation, or using relaxation techniques.

- **Seeking Help When Needed:** Encourage your child to seek help from a trusted adult, like a teacher or parent, if they feel overwhelmed or unable to resolve a conflict on their own.

- By developing these skills, your child becomes better equipped to navigate social challenges, resolve conflicts constructively, and build stronger, more resilient friendships.

In the next Part we'll delves deeper into the world of self-awareness and self-regulation, empowering your child to manage their emotions and navigate life's challenges with confidence.

PART 4

ENHANCING LEARNING AND
EDUCATION: EQUIPPING YOUR CHILD
FOR SUCCESS

Education unlocks a world of possibilities. This section equips you with the tools to navigate the educational landscape and ensure your child thrives in the classroom and beyond. Here, you'll discover:

Effective Advocacy: Learn how to understand and utilize Individualized Education Plans (IEPs) to secure the right support for your child's unique needs.

Engaging Strategies: Explore effective teaching methods that cater to the learning styles of children with high-functioning autism, fostering engagement and academic success.

Building a Strong Foundation: Discover strategies to support your child's learning journey both inside and outside the classroom, creating a strong foundation for lifelong learning.

Get ready to become your child's champion, advocating for their needs and empowering them to reach their full academic potential!

CHAPTER 8: UNLOCKING YOUR CHILD'S POTENTIAL: A GUIDE TO IEPS AND EFFECTIVE TEACHING STRATEGIES

Education is a powerful tool that empowers your child to explore, learn, and grow. This chapter equips you with the knowledge and strategies to navigate the educational system and unlock your child's full potential. Here, we delve into two crucial areas:

- *Understanding and Utilizing Individualized Education Plans (IEPs):*
- *Exploring Effective Teaching Strategies for Children with High-Functioning Autism*

8.1 Understanding IEPs and Advocating for Your Child's Needs: Securing the Right Support

An Individualized Education Plan (IEP) is a roadmap to success, outlining the specific academic goals and supports your child needs to thrive in school. Understanding IEPs and advocating for your child's unique needs is crucial for their academic journey. Here's what you'll learn:

- **The IEP Process:** This section demystifies the IEP process, explaining the roles of different team members, timelines, and what to expect during IEP meetings.

- **Identifying Your Child's Needs:** Learn how to collaborate with teachers and specialists to identify your child's strengths, weaknesses, and specific learning needs related to autism.

- **Setting SMART Goals:** Discover how to set Specific, Measurable, Achievable, Relevant, and Time-bound goals within the IEP that cater to your child's individual learning style and development.

- **Advocacy in Action:** This section equips you with communication skills and strategies to advocate for your child's needs during IEP meetings. Learn how to effectively express your concerns, ask questions, and ensure the IEP reflects your child's best interests.

8.2 *Effective Teaching Strategies for Children with High-Functioning Autism: Engaging and Empowering Learners*

Every child learns differently. This section explores teaching strategies specifically tailored to support children with high-functioning autism, fostering engagement and academic success:

- **Visual Aids and Organization:** Visual schedules, graphic organizers, and clear instructions are essential tools for children with autism. These provide a roadmap for learning and help them stay organized.

- **Differentiation:** No two learners are alike. This section explores differentiation strategies, where teachers adapt instruction and materials to cater to your child's unique learning style and pace.

- **Multisensory Learning:** Engaging multiple senses (auditory, visual, kinesthetic) can enhance learning for children with autism. Explore strategies that incorporate movement, hands-on activities, and technology into the learning process.

- **Social-Emotional Learning (SEL):** Social interaction and emotional regulation are crucial skills for success in school and life. Explore how teachers can integrate SEL activities into the curriculum to help your child develop these essential skills.

- **Positive Reinforcement and Collaboration:** Positive reinforcement motivates your child and fosters a love of learning. This section emphasizes collaboration between teachers, parents, and therapists to ensure consistent support and celebrate your child's progress.

8.3 *Supporting Academic Success in the Classroom and Beyond: Building a Strong Foundation for Learning*

Your child's learning journey extends beyond the classroom walls. This section explores strategies to create a supportive learning environment at home and empower your child to become an active participant in their education:

- **Open Communication and Collaboration:** Maintain open communication with your child's teachers and collaborate on strategies that can be implemented both at school and home. This consistency reinforces learning and helps your child feel supported.

- **Creating a Sensory-Friendly Learning Environment:** Adapt your home environment to minimize sensory overload and create a designated study space that promotes focus and concentration.

- **Organization and Time Management Skills:** Help your child develop organizational skills and time management strategies to manage homework, projects, and daily routines effectively.

- **Self-Advocacy Skills:** Empower your child to self-advocate for their needs in the classroom. This could involve communicating with teachers when they need clarification on instructions or requesting breaks when feeling overwhelmed.

- **Building Independence and Confidence:** As your child progresses, encourage them to take ownership of their learning. This fosters independence, confidence, and a lifelong love of exploration and discovery.

By understanding IEPs, advocating for your child's needs, and utilizing effective teaching strategies, you create a powerful support system that unlocks your child's potential and paves the way for academic success.

In the next page we'll delves into the world of self-awareness and self-regulation, empowering your child to manage their emotions and navigate social situations with confidence.

PART 5

BUILDING RESILIENCE AND COPING SKILLS: EMPOWERING YOUR CHILD TO NAVIGATE CHALLENGES

Life throws curveballs, and for children with high-functioning autism, navigating these challenges can sometimes feel overwhelming. This section equips you with tools to empower your child. Here, you'll discover strategies to help them:

- **Identify and understand their emotions:** Become a detective of their inner world, helping them recognize and name their feelings.

- **Develop healthy coping mechanisms:** Equip your child with a toolbox of strategies to manage frustration, anxiety, and emotional overwhelm effectively.

- **Build resilience and self-esteem:** Foster the inner strength and confidence your child needs to navigate challenges and bounce back from setbacks.

- Get ready to become your child's emotional cheerleader, equipping them with the skills to navigate life's complexities with confidence and a positive outlook!

CHAPTER 9: BUILDING EMOTIONAL RESILIENCE: DEVELOPING HEALTHY COPING MECHANISMS

Life is a rollercoaster of emotions, and for children with high-functioning autism, navigating these emotional ups and downs can be particularly challenging. This chapter equips you with tools to empower your child to develop emotional resilience and build a toolbox of coping mechanisms.

9.1 Recognizing and Understanding Emotions: Helping Your Child Identify Their Feelings

The first step to managing emotions effectively is recognizing them. Many children with autism struggle to identify their internal states. This section explores strategies to help your child become a detective of their inner world:

- **The Language of Emotions:** Expand your child's emotional vocabulary. Create charts with pictures or use emotion recognition games to identify happy, sad, angry, frustrated, and other emotions.

- **Connecting Emotions to Physical Cues:** Many emotions manifest physically. Help your child recognize these cues. A racing heart might indicate anxiety, sweaty palms could signal frustration, and tightness in the chest could be a sign of sadness.

- **Journaling and Reflective Activities:** Encourage journaling or creating visual representations of their emotions. Drawing a happy face when they feel content or a stormy cloud when they're upset allows your child to explore their inner world and understand their emotional responses to different situations.

9.2 *Healthy Coping Mechanisms for Managing Frustration and Anxiety: Equipping Your Child with Tools for Success*

Once your child recognizes their emotions, it's time to develop healthy strategies for managing them, particularly strong emotions like frustration and anxiety. This section explores a toolkit of coping mechanisms:

- **Calming Techniques:** Equip your child with calming techniques like deep breathing exercises, mindfulness practices, or progressive muscle relaxation. Practice these techniques regularly so they become second nature when emotions run high.

- **Sensory Tools:** Sensory overload can be a significant trigger for emotional outbursts. Provide your child with sensory tools like fidget toys, weighted blankets, or noise-canceling headphones.

These tools can offer comfort and help them manage overwhelming sensory input.

- **Identifying Triggers:** Work together to identify situations or stimuli that trigger strong emotions. Knowing their triggers allows you to develop proactive strategies to avoid these triggers or manage them effectively.

- **Positive Self-Talk:** Help your child develop positive self-talk to combat negative emotions and self-doubt. Encourage them to use affirmations like "I can handle this" or "I'm going to take a deep breath and calm down" when feeling overwhelmed.

9.3 *Building Emotional Resilience and Self-Esteem: Empowering Your Child to Thrive*

Building emotional resilience is about bouncing back from challenges and setbacks. This section explores strategies to foster resilience and self-esteem in your child:

- **Celebrating Milestones (Big and Small):** Acknowledge and celebrate your child's progress, no matter how seemingly insignificant. Did they use a calming technique to manage frustration? Did they express their emotions in a healthy way? Celebrating these efforts builds self-esteem and motivates them to continue learning.

- **Open Communication and Support:** Maintain open communication and create a safe space for your child to express their emotions and challenges.

Your understanding and support are crucial for building resilience. Let them know you're there for them, no matter what.

- **Focus on Strengths:** Help your child identify their strengths and talents. Focusing on their abilities builds confidence and empowers them to navigate challenges with a positive outlook. Remind them of their past successes to fuel their self-belief.

By fostering emotional awareness, providing coping mechanisms, and building resilience, you equip your child with the tools they need to navigate life's complexities with confidence and a positive outlook.

Remember, this journey is a marathon, not a sprint. Celebrate progress, focus on building skills, and empower your child to become the architect of their own emotional well-being.

PART 6

TRANSITIONING TO ADULTHOOD: LAUNCHING WITH CONFIDENCE

Adulthood beckons! This section equips you and your child with the tools for a smooth and successful transition. Here, you'll explore crucial aspects of preparing for this exciting new chapter:

Charting the Course: We'll delve into exploring post-secondary education options and potential career paths that align with your child's unique strengths and interests.

Building Independence: Developing essential independent living skills and self-advocacy tools empowers your child to thrive as an adult.

Building a Support Network: Discover strategies for creating a strong support system that will ensure your child feels empowered and supported as they venture into adulthood.

Get ready to celebrate your child's growth and prepare them to launch confidently into a bright future!

CHAPTER 10: CHARTING THE COURSE: PREPARING FOR A SUCCESSFUL TRANSITION

The transition to adulthood is a significant milestone for any young person, and for those with high-functioning autism, it can be both exciting and daunting. This chapter equips you and your child with the tools to navigate this crucial period and ensure a smooth and successful launch into adulthood. Here, we'll explore three key areas to chart a course for a fulfilling future:

10.1 Exploring Post-Secondary Education Options and Career Paths: Mapping the Future

Education opens doors to opportunity. This section delves into the exciting world of post-secondary education and career exploration:

- **Understanding Options:** Explore the diverse landscape of post-secondary education, including traditional four-year colleges, community colleges, vocational training programs, and gap year opportunities. Consider your child's strengths, interests, and learning style when making this crucial decision.

- **Career Exploration:** Help your child identify potential career paths that align with their passions, skills, and personality. Utilize career assessments, informational interviews with professionals in fields of interest, and job shadowing opportunities to gain valuable insights.

- **Transition Planning:** Many high schools offer transition planning programs to assist students with disabilities in preparing for college or the workforce.

These programs can be invaluable resources for guidance and support.

10.2 Developing Independent Living Skills and Self-Advocacy: Empowering Your Child for Adulthood

Independence is a cornerstone of adulthood. This section focuses on equipping your child with the essential skills to navigate daily life:

- **Life Skills Training:** Develop a plan to teach your child essential life skills such as budgeting, time management, cooking, personal hygiene, and laundry. Break down these skills into smaller, manageable steps and celebrate milestones along the way.

- **Self-Advocacy Skills:** Empower your child to speak up for their needs and communicate effectively.

Role-play scenarios where they might need to self-advocate, such as requesting accommodations in a college setting or asking for help at work.

- **Transportation:** Explore transportation options and help your child develop the skills necessary to navigate public transportation systems or obtain a driver's license if desired.

10.3 Building a Support Network for Adulthood: Securing a Strong Foundation for the Future

No one thrives in isolation. This section emphasizes the importance of building a strong support network for your child:

- **Identifying Resources:** Explore resources available to adults with autism, including support groups, government services, and mentorship programs.

- **Family Communication:** Maintain open communication with your child and discuss their needs and preferences for ongoing support as they transition to adulthood.

- **Building Relationships:** Encourage your child to build and maintain healthy relationships with friends, family members, and mentors. A strong support network provides a sense of belonging and ensures your child feels connected and supported.

By proactively planning for post-secondary education, fostering independent living skills, and building a strong support network, you empower your child to navigate the exciting journey of adulthood with confidence and self-determination.

In the next Part we'll delves into the importance of celebrating achievements, embracing neurodiversity, and fostering long-term well-being.

PART 7

CELEBRATING YOUR CHILD'S REMARKABLE ADVENTURES

Raising a child with high-functioning autism is a unique and rewarding experience. This final section serves as a heartwarming reminder to cherish the journey and celebrate your child's remarkable growth. Here, you'll explore:

- **The power of celebrating milestones:** Learn how acknowledging achievements, big and small, fuels your child's confidence and self-esteem.

- **Embracing neurodiversity:** Discover the beauty of appreciating the unique strengths and perspectives that autism brings to your child's life.

- **Building on success for a fulfilling future:** Explore strategies to sustain progress and empower your child to live a happy and fulfilling life.

This chapter serves as a warm embrace, reminding you to cherish the victories, celebrate the individuality, and embrace the ongoing journey with your extraordinary child.

CHAPTER 11: CELEBRATING SUCCESS AND GROWTH: EMBRACING YOUR CHILD'S JOURNEY

Raising a child with high-functioning autism is an adventure filled with unique challenges and triumphs. This chapter serves as a warm embrace, reminding you to celebrate the victories, big and small, and cherish the remarkable journey you've shared with your extraordinary child.

11.1 Recognizing Achievements and Milestones: Celebrating Every Step of the Way

Our children thrive on encouragement and recognition. This section explores the power of celebrating achievements and milestones:

- **The Importance of Celebration:** Acknowledging even seemingly insignificant progress reinforces positive behavior and motivates your child to continue learning and growing. Celebrate mastering a new skill, conquering a fear, or simply trying something new.

- **Finding Joy in the Everyday:** Everyday moments hold opportunities for celebration. Did your child overcome a sensory overload at the grocery store? Did they ask for help when needed? Celebrate these victories – they pave the way for future success.

- **Building Confidence:** Recognition and celebration fuel your child's confidence and self-esteem. As they see themselves as capable and successful, they are more likely to embrace challenges and persevere through difficulties.

11.2 *Embracing Neurodiversity and Individuality: The Power of Being Unique*

Autism is not a deficit, but a unique way of experiencing the world. This section delves into the power of embracing neurodiversity:

- **Celebrating Strengths:** Your child possesses unique strengths and talents. Perhaps they have an exceptional memory, a keen eye for detail, or a passion for a particular subject. Celebrate these strengths and encourage their exploration.

- **Understanding Differences:** Autism shapes how your child interacts with the world. Embrace these differences and focus on fostering communication and understanding.

- **The Beauty of Being Unique:** Neurodiversity enriches the world.

Celebrate your child's unique perspective and individuality.

11.3 Sustaining Progress for a Fulfilling Future: Building on Success

The journey doesn't end here. This section explores strategies to sustain progress and empower your child for a fulfilling future:

- **Maintaining Support Systems:** The support network you've built will continue to be crucial. Maintain connections with therapists, mentors, and educators as your child moves forward.

- **Lifelong Learning:** Learning is a lifelong journey. Encourage your child to embrace new challenges, explore their interests, and continue developing their skills.

- **Setting Realistic Goals:** Work with your child to set realistic and achievable goals.

Celebrate milestones along the way, and remember that progress, not perfection, is the key.

By cherishing the victories, celebrating individuality, and fostering ongoing growth, you empower your child to navigate life with confidence and embrace the exciting possibilities that lie ahead.

Remember, you are not alone on this journey. There are countless resources and a supportive community to guide you every step of the way.

CONCLUSION

CHAPTER 12: A LIFELONG PATH: EMPOWERING YOUR CHILD'S FUTURE

The journey of raising a child with high-functioning autism is a beautiful tapestry woven with challenges, triumphs, and moments of immense pride. As you reach the end of this book, remember, the story is far from over. This chapter serves as a warm embrace, reminding you of the invaluable takeaways from this journey and offering a glimpse into the exciting future that awaits your child.

Reflecting on the Journey:

- **Celebrating Growth:** Revisit the significant milestones your child has achieved. From mastering academic skills to developing independent living abilities and navigating social situations, acknowledge their growth and celebrate their resilience.

- **Embracing Individuality:** Remember the unique strengths and perspectives your child brings to the world. Their way of experiencing life enriches your own and contributes a valuable lens to the world around us.

- **The Power of Support:** Recognize the invaluable support system you've built. From dedicated educators to therapists, family, and friends, acknowledge their role in your child's journey and reach out for continued support as needed.

- **Empowering Your Child's Future:**

- **Advocacy in Action:** As your child enters adulthood, continue to be their advocate. Help them navigate college applications, job interviews, or any situation where they might need assistance in asserting their needs and rights.

- **Lifelong Learning:** Encourage your child's passion for lifelong learning. Help them find resources for exploring their interests, developing new skills, and continuing their intellectual growth.

- **Building Confidence:** Fuel your child's self-esteem by fostering independence and encouraging them to take ownership of their decisions. Celebrate their successes, acknowledge setbacks as learning opportunities, and remind them of their inherent strengths and capabilities.

Looking Forward with Hope:

As your child transitions to adulthood, a world brimming with possibilities awaits.

Remember, they are not defined by their diagnosis. They are a unique individual with talents, passions, and dreams. The skills and knowledge you've equipped them with are the building blocks for a fulfilling future.

This book may be closing, but your journey continues. Hold onto the lessons learned, cherish the moments shared, and embrace the exciting adventures that lie ahead. The future is bright for your child, and you are their unwavering champion every step of the way.

APPENDIX

This appendix provides additional resources to support your journey in raising a child with high-functioning autism.

GLOSSARY OF KEY TERMS

This glossary defines key terms encountered throughout the book:

- **Applied Behavior Analysis (ABA):** An evidence-based therapy approach that uses positive reinforcement to teach new skills and improve behaviors.

- **Asperger Syndrome:** A term no longer included in the diagnostic criteria for autism, but sometimes used to describe individuals with autism who have average or above average cognitive abilities and may not experience significant delays in speech development.

- **Diagnostic and Statistical Manual (DSM-5):** The manual used by mental health professionals to diagnose mental disorders, including autism spectrum disorder (ASD).

- **Executive Functioning Skills:** Mental processes such as planning, organization, time management, and problem-solving.

- **High-Functioning Autism:** A term used to describe individuals on the autism spectrum who have average or above average cognitive abilities and may have some challenges with social interaction and communication.

- **Individualized Education Program (IEP):** A legal document outlining a child's specific learning needs and the supports they require to succeed in school.

- **Neurodiversity:** The idea that the human brain comes in a wide variety of types, and that these variations are not deficits but different ways of functioning.

- **Sensory Processing Disorder (SPD):** A condition where the brain has difficulty processing sensory information from the environment.

- **Self-Advocacy:** The ability to speak up for oneself and one's needs.

- **Social-Emotional Learning (SEL):** The process of acquiring and applying the knowledge, skills, and attitudes to understand and manage emotions, set and achieve positive goals, establish and maintain positive relationships, and make responsible decisions.

- **Spectrum Disorder:** A term used to describe a condition that can manifest in a wide range of ways, with varying degrees of severity.

BONUS CHAPTER

BENNY'S COLORFUL WORLD: A STORY ABOUT FRIENDSHIP

OPEN YOUR EYES TO A WORLD BURSTING WITH COLOR!

Welcome to Benny's Colorful World, where everything shimmers brighter and details pop like fireworks. Here lives Benny, a curious kid who sees the world in a way all his own. But sometimes, the bustling playground feels like a cacophony of sounds and the crowded classroom a whirlwind of activity.

That's where Maya comes in! Join these two amazing friends as they embark on a heartwarming adventure. Maya's kindness and understanding help Benny navigate the world's bright lights and bustling sounds. Together, they build a spectacular treehouse, not just with wood and cardboard, but with friendship and acceptance.

Benny's Colorful World: A Story About Friendship is more than just a tale. It's a vibrant exploration of how different perspectives can create extraordinary friendships. It's about celebrating what makes us unique and finding the joy in seeing the world through someone else's eyes.

Are you ready to step into Benny's colorful world? Let's turn the page and discover a world of friendship, acceptance, and imagination!

*Seeing the World Through Rainbow Glasses:
Understanding Differences*

Benny loved the world! But for him, it wasn't just a world of red, green, and blue. It was a dazzling explosion of color! When he looked at a tree, he saw every shade of green imaginable, emerald leaves shimmering next to deep, mossy trunks. Sometimes, it felt like he was wearing a pair of magical rainbow glasses, making everything burst with vibrant life.

There were times, though, when the world seemed a little too much. The school hallways were a noisy tunnel of sound, and the bustling playground felt like a swirling kaleidoscope. This is where things were a little different for Benny. Some people, like Benny, have autism. It's a kind of superpower that makes them see and hear things in special ways, sometimes in ways that can be overwhelming.

But guess what? Having autism comes with amazing strengths too! Just like Benny's incredible eye for detail, which helped him notice the tiniest insects crawling on the playground or the most beautiful patterns in the clouds. This kind of focus can be a superpower when it comes to learning and doing things you love.

So, the next time you meet someone who sees the world a little differently, remember, they might just be wearing a pair of invisible rainbow glasses, ready to show you the world in a whole new light!

Building a Bridge of Friendship: Kindness and Understanding

One sunny afternoon, a new student named Maya joined Benny's class. While the other kids were a little shy around Benny, Maya scooted right next to him with a friendly smile.

She noticed how Benny seemed fascinated by the patterns on the classroom ceiling, his eyes wide with focus. Remembering Benny might see the world a little differently, Maya gently asked, "Hey Benny, do you like looking at the shapes up there?"

Benny, surprised by her friendly voice, turned to Maya and nodded eagerly. He started pointing out intricate details in the ceiling tiles that Maya hadn't noticed before. They talked about the different shapes and colors, and Maya realized Benny saw the world in a truly amazing way.

This simple conversation opened a bridge of friendship. Communication is like building a bridge, it allows us to connect with others and share our thoughts and feelings. Maya understood that sometimes, all it takes is a kind question or a shared interest to start a beautiful friendship.

As the days turned into weeks, Maya learned that Benny loved building things with incredible precision. He could take a pile of blocks and create amazing structures, towers that seemed to defy gravity! However, sometimes the noisy classroom environment made it hard for Benny to concentrate. One day, during a particularly loud assembly, Maya noticed Benny starting to feel overwhelmed. Without saying a word, she offered him a reassuring smile and pointed to a quiet corner near the library.

Benny felt a wave of relief wash over him. Maya understood! He knew she didn't mind that he saw the world a little differently.

In that quiet corner, they continued building imaginary worlds using blocks and their imaginations, their friendship growing stronger with every shared creation.

Maya and Benny celebrated each other's differences. Maya appreciated Benny's incredible focus and attention to detail, while Benny learned to enjoy the world's sounds and social interactions with Maya by his side. Their friendship blossomed because they didn't try to change each other, but instead, embraced what made each of them unique.

A World Too Loud: Sensory Overload and a Helping Hand

Recess time was usually Benny's favorite part of the day. He loved building elaborate structures in the sandbox and soaring high on the swings. But today, something felt different. The shouts of children playing tag echoed off the brick walls like a hundred barking dogs. The rhythmic bouncing of basketballs on the court vibrated through his bones, and the colorful plastic toys scattered across the ground seemed to pulsate in the bright sunlight.

Benny's world, usually a symphony of vibrant colors and fascinating details, had become a chaotic cacophony. This overwhelming flood of sights and sounds was a common experience for Benny, a result of sensory sensitivities that came with his autism. It felt like his brain was overflowing with information, making it hard to focus or relax.

Just as Benny started to feel overwhelmed, a gentle hand touched his shoulder. It was Maya. She noticed Benny's furrowed brow and the way he was clenching his fists. Remembering what she had learned about autism, Maya understood that the noisy playground might be a bit too much for him right now.

"Hey Benny," Maya whispered kindly, "Would you like to find a quieter spot?"

Benny looked at her, a flicker of relief crossing his face. He nodded slowly, unable to form the words caught in his throat. Maya smiled reassuringly and led him away from the commotion, towards a quiet corner of the library near a large bookshelf.

The library felt like a cool, calming oasis compared to the bustling playground. Sunlight filtered through the window, casting soft shadows across the floor. Maya pointed to a comfy beanbag chair tucked away in the corner. "This is my favorite spot to read," she said softly. "Do you want to sit here?"

Benny sank into the beanbag, the soft embrace instantly calming his racing heart. He focused on the gentle hum of the air conditioner and the rhythmic tick of the grandfather clock in the corner. The world seemed to slow down; the overwhelming chaos replaced by a comforting sense of quiet.

Taking a deep breath, a technique they had been practicing in class, Benny felt a wave of tension ease from his shoulders. He looked at Maya with a grateful smile. She had understood his need for quiet without needing him to explain. In that moment, Benny knew their friendship was something special.

Unlocking Communication: Understanding Social Cues and Building Bridges

School lunches were another time that sometimes felt tricky for Benny. He loved the delicious smells wafting from the cafeteria, but the crowded tables and loud chatter often left him feeling overwhelmed. He preferred to sit alone, quietly enjoying his food while lost in his own thoughts.

One day, as Benny sat at the far corner table, Maya noticed him fiddling with his lunchbox, his brow furrowed.

Unlike his usual enthusiastic chatter about the fascinating patterns on his apple, Benny seemed withdrawn. Subtle social cues, like body language and facial expressions, could sometimes be a bit of a mystery for Benny.

Maya understood that Benny might be feeling a bit lonely. She wanted to invite him to join her table, but she also knew it wouldn't be helpful to overwhelm him. Thinking for a moment, Maya grabbed her own lunch and walked over to Benny's table with a friendly smile.

"Hey Benny," she said cheerfully, "Mind if I join you for a bit? I found this amazing book about insects and I wanted to show you the pictures!"

Benny, surprised but happy by the invitation, nodded eagerly. He loved anything related to nature and insects, especially the intricate patterns on their wings.

As Maya opened the book, sharing the fascinating details with genuine excitement, Benny's initial apprehension melted away.

Their shared interest in insects sparked a lively conversation. Benny pointed out the detailed patterns on an ant's leg he noticed in the picture, while Maya explained the different types of camouflage some insects used. Lunchtime, once a solitary experience, became a space for shared knowledge and joyful discovery.

This wasn't the only time Maya initiated activities to bridge the social gap. Remember the rainy afternoon stuck indoors? While some kids might have grumbled about being stuck inside, Maya saw an opportunity for something special.

With a mischievous glint in her eye, she turned to Benny and whispered, "Hey, have you ever seen a treehouse made of cardboard?" Knowing Benny's love for building and his incredible focus, it was an invitation perfectly tailored to his unique interests.

The cardboard castle project wasn't just about creating a cool structure. It was a beautiful display of social interaction and shared enjoyment. Together, they communicated, collaborated, and celebrated each other's strengths.

Benny, with his meticulous planning, ensured every piece fit perfectly, while Maya's enthusiasm kept them motivated.

As other children shyly approached, curious about their cardboard masterpiece, Benny and Maya didn't hesitate to include them.

They learned that communication could be more than words, it could be a language of shared interests and collaborative building. They built not just a treehouse, but a bridge of understanding and acceptance.

The joy on all their faces as they explored their cardboard creation solidified the importance of social interaction. It wasn't about forcing conversations or changing personalities, but about creating a space where everyone felt included and their unique strengths were celebrated.

A World of Colors: Celebrating Neurodiversity in the Cardboard Castle

The rainy afternoon, once a potential source of frustration, had transformed into a masterpiece of creativity. Benny, fueled by Maya's invitation, had unleashed his incredible spatial awareness.

His mind, a master of detail and construction, whirred with blueprints. He meticulously sketched the treehouse design on a discarded piece of paper, careful consideration given to every nook and cranny.

As they gathered discarded cardboard boxes, Benny's focus was laser-sharp. Maya watched in awe as he transformed flat cardboard into walls, floors, and even a lookout tower designed for optimal view. It was more than just a structure; it was a testament to Benny's unique way of seeing the world, a world where details held immense importance.

The construction process became a celebration of their differences. Maya's boundless energy kept them motivated, while Benny's meticulous approach ensured every piece fit perfectly. The cardboard castle wasn't just a physical structure; it was a bridge between their unique perspectives.

Once their cardboard masterpiece stood proudly in the classroom corner, Benny, emboldened by Maya's acceptance, used markers to paint the outside. He wasn't just adding color; he was translating his vibrant world onto the cardboard walls. Spirals and swirls danced across the surface, reflecting the kaleidoscope of colors that filled Benny's vision.

Inside, Maya added comfy cushions and books, transforming it into a haven for them to escape to, if needed. But the true magic unfolded when other classmates, curious about this magnificent cardboard castle, started approaching.

Benny and Maya, no longer hesitant about their differences, welcomed them in with open arms. They shared stories about their building process, Benny explaining how he designed the lookout tower to maximize the view, a detail that would have escaped most others.

As the once-isolated corner became a hub of activity, a beautiful realization dawned. Their friendship, built on acceptance and celebration of differences, had opened a door for understanding. Other children, inspired by Benny's unique perspective and Maya's kindness, started adding their own touches to the cardboard treehouse. It became a testament to neurodiversity and the magic that happens when different viewpoints come together.

The cardboard castle wasn't just a temporary refuge; it was a symbol of a world where everyone is celebrated for their unique way of seeing things. Benny's colorful world, once a solitary place, bloomed into a vibrant shared experience.

Benny's Colorful World reminds us that true friendship embraces differences.

It's about celebrating the strengths of neurodiversity and the beauty of seeing the world through a kaleidoscope of unique lenses. So, open your eyes wide and embrace the magic that unfolds when we celebrate what makes each of us special. After all, the world might be a cacophony of sounds and a kaleidoscope of colors, but together, we can create a symphony of acceptance and a masterpiece of friendship.

A WORLD OF FRIENDSHIP AND ACCEPTANCE: WRAPPING UP BENNY'S COLORFUL JOURNEY

Benny's Colorful World takes us on a heartwarming adventure of friendship and understanding. We join Benny, a curious boy who sees the world in a vibrant explosion of color, and Maya, his kind and accepting friend.

Throughout the story, we learn valuable lessons about:

- Understanding Differences: We discover that people like Benny experience the world differently, sometimes with heightened sensitivities or a focus on intricate details. However, these differences are not something to be afraid of, but rather strengths to be celebrated.

- Building Friendship: Communication and kindness are the cornerstones of a strong friendship. Maya's willingness to understand Benny's needs and offer a helping hand paves the way for a beautiful connection.

- Sensory Sensitivities: The story sheds light on the challenges of sensory overload that can sometimes come with autism. We see how a quiet space or a calming technique can make a big difference for someone feeling overwhelmed.

- Social Interactions: Not everything about friendship needs to be spelled out verbally. Shared interests, like building a cardboard treehouse, can be an invitation for connection and joyful experiences.

- Celebrating Neurodiversity: Ultimately, "Benny's Colorful World" is a celebration of neurodiversity.

It reminds us that every mind is unique, and our differences are what make our world so rich and vibrant.

By embracing friendship, understanding, and acceptance, Benny and Maya create their own little masterpiece a cardboard castle that stands as a symbol of a world where everyone feels included and celebrated for who they are.

So, the next time you encounter someone who sees the world a little differently, remember Benny and his colorful world. Open your heart and mind to the beauty of neurodiversity, and you might just discover a whole new way of seeing the world yourself.

Q & A AND LOOKING FORWARD

This bonus chapter offers an opportunity to delve deeper into some key questions and provide a glimpse into the future of autism awareness and support.

Q: This book has been a tremendous resource for our family. Are there any other resources you recommend?

Absolutely! Here are a few starting points to continue your journey:

Websites:

- Autism Speaks: https://www.autismspeaks.org/
- The National Autistic Society: https://www.autism.org.uk/

- Understood.org:
  https://www.understood.org/en/articles/what -is-autism

Organizations:

- Autism Society of America: https://autismsociety.org/
- The Arc: https://thearc.org/
- The Autistic Self Advocacy Network: https://autisticadvocacy.org/

Q: My child struggles with [specific challenge, e.g., making eye contact]. Do you have any suggestions?

This is a common challenge for many individuals with autism. The book may have already addressed general social communication strategies, but here are some additional tips for making eye contact:

- **Start with short intervals:** Encourage brief eye contact during preferred activities.

- **Use visual supports:** Practice making eye contact with pictures or videos before moving on to real people.

- **Positive reinforcement:** Acknowledge and celebrate even small improvements.

Q: What are some of the biggest misconceptions about autism that you'd like to address?

One common misconception is that autism is a form of intellectual disability. However, many individuals with autism have average or above average cognitive abilities. Another misconception is that all people with autism are nonverbal. While some individuals may be nonverbal, many others have varying degrees of communication ability.

Q: What does the future hold for individuals with high-functioning autism?

The future for individuals with HFA is bright! There's a growing understanding and acceptance of autism in society. Research is ongoing, leading to advancements in diagnosis, support, and interventions. With proper support, individuals with HFA can achieve their full potential and lead fulfilling lives.

Q: What words of encouragement would you offer parents raising a child with autism?

Raising a child with autism is a remarkable journey filled with unique challenges and triumphs. Remember, your child is an individual with incredible strengths, talents, and a unique way of experiencing the world. Celebrate their individuality, embrace their differences, and empower them to reach their full potential.

There is a supportive community of parents, educators, and professionals on this journey with you.

Looking Forward:

As research and understanding of autism spectrum disorder continues to grow, the future holds immense promise for individuals with HFA. Early intervention, combined with ongoing support and acceptance, will empower these remarkable individuals to thrive in all aspects of life.

Interactive Activity:

Understanding Your Child's Sensory Needs:

Sensory processing challenges are a common experience for individuals with autism. This brief self-assessment can help you identify areas where your child might require additional support:

Instructions:

Read each statement and rate how often it applies to your child using a scale of 1 (never) to 5 (always).

- My child seems bothered by loud noises like sirens or crowded places. ( )
- They dislike certain textures of clothing or prefer loose-fitting garments. ( )
- Bright lights or flickering screens seem to irritate them. ( )
- They have a strong sense of smell and might be sensitive to certain odors. ( )
- My child seeks out repetitive movements or enjoys fidget toys. ( )

Scoring:

A score of 15 or higher suggests your child might have some sensory processing sensitivities. It's important to note that this is not a diagnostic tool and consulting a healthcare professional is recommended for a comprehensive evaluation.

Additional Resources:

The following resources offer in-depth information on sensory processing and strategies to support individuals with sensory sensitivities:

- https://www.understood.org/en/articles/what-is-autism
- https://www.autismspeaks.org/sensory-issues

OPEN ENDED QUESTIONS:

Q: Throughout this book, you've emphasized the importance of celebrating our child's achievements. Can you share some specific ways to do this?

Absolutely! Celebrating achievements, big and small, reinforces positive behavior and motivates your child to continue learning and growing. Here are some ideas:

- **Acknowledge effort and progress:** Not everything comes easily. Celebrate their perseverance and the steps they take towards a goal.

- **Create a reward system:** Establish a reward system based on achieving milestones or completing tasks.

- **Public praise (if appropriate):** Some children thrive on public recognition.

Celebrate their accomplishments in front of family or friends (always with their permission).

- **Focus on their interests:** Celebrate achievements related to their hobbies and passions. This shows you value their individuality.

Q: This book has focused on parents, but what about siblings of children with autism?

Siblings play a vital role in a child's life, and having a brother or sister with autism can be a unique experience. Here are some resources specifically for siblings:

- The Sibling Society: https://siblingsupport.org/connect/
- Understood.org: https://medium.com/equality-includes-

you/empathy-in-action-how-to-support-asd-
siblings-3efd33141210

We hope this bonus chapter has provided valuable insights and additional resources for your journey. Remember, you are not alone. There is a supportive community and a bright future ahead for your child with high-functioning autism.